Nelson

ENGLISH

DEVELOPMENT

BOOK 1

JOHN JACKMAN

WENDY WREN

Nelson

D0453012

Contents

Stimulus	Writing	Working with Words
modern poetry illustrations	sentence completion lists imaginative/descriptive poetry – acrostic classifying	matching – animal homes
photograph non-fiction famous painting picture story illustrations	finish the story descriptive lists	classifying – cat family
plan rules illustrations	descriptive (personal) analysing rules sentence writing	compound words
traditional verse illustrations diagram	lists descriptive personal diagram	homophones – weather
famous painting illustrations	descriptive lists	adjectives – colour
modern poetry illustrations modern fiction	descriptive sentence writing personal lists	adjectives – sounds
non-fiction illustrations photographs modern fiction	personal/descriptive lists finish the story	looking at languages – Chinese numbers
modern fiction illustrations photographs	matching text/pictures personal sentence writing sentence completion	classifying – house
modern poetry illustrations	personal sentence writing matching text/pictures	word groups
non-fiction map/diagram photograph illustrations	instructions diagram imaginative letter-writing	looking at languages – Roman numerals
legend illustrations poster	imaginative personal descriptive poster	looking at languages – Anglo-Saxon

Where do animals live?

Rabbit and Lark

'Under the ground
  It's rumbly and dark
And interesting,'
  Said Rabbit to Lark.

Said Lark to Rabbit
  'Up in the sky
There's plenty of room
  And it's airy and high.'

'Under the ground
  It's warm and dry
Won't you live with me?'
  Was Rabbit's reply.

'There's air so sunny
  I wish you'd agree,'
Said the little Lark,
  'To live with me.'

But under the ground
  And up in the sky,
Larks can't burrow
  Nor rabbits fly.

So skylark over
  And rabbit under
They had to settle
  to live asunder.

And often these two friends
  Meet with a will
For a chat together
  On top of the hill.

James Reeves

Glossary: a *glossary* explains what a word means
asunder means apart
meet with a will means happy to see each other

COMPREHENSION   Now you have read the poem answer the questions.

1   Find the words that tell you what it is like underground.

2   Find the words that tell you what it is like in the sky.

3   Why can't the rabbit live in the sky?

4   Why can't the skylark live underground?

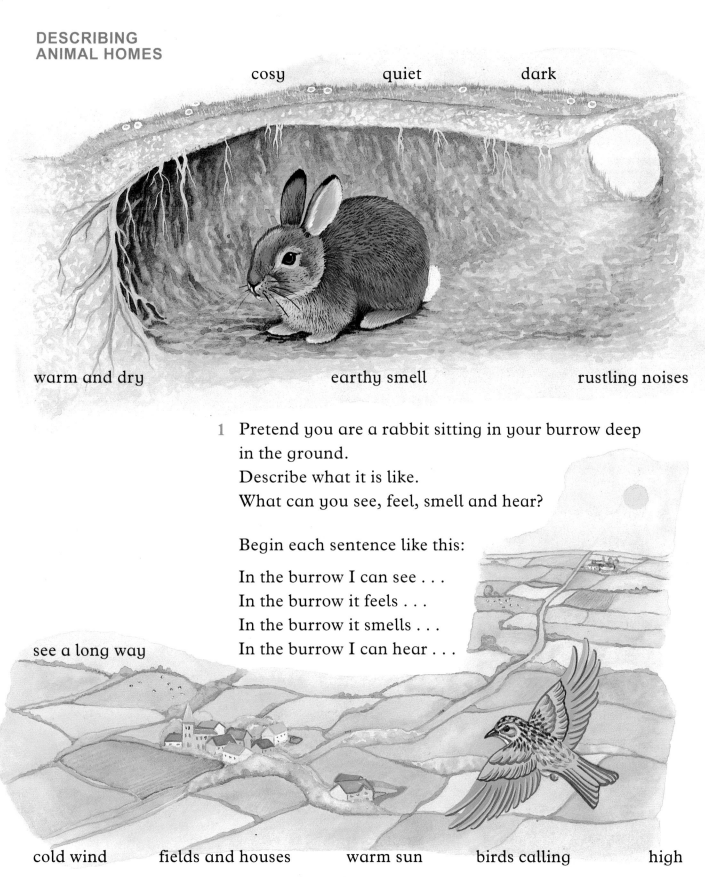

cosy   quiet   dark

warm and dry   earthy smell   rustling noises

1 Pretend you are a rabbit sitting in your burrow deep
in the ground.
Describe what it is like.
What can you see, feel, smell and hear?

Begin each sentence like this:

In the burrow I can see . . .
In the burrow it feels . . .
In the burrow it smells . . .
In the burrow I can hear . . .

see a long way

cold wind   fields and houses   warm sun   birds calling   high

2 Now pretend you are a bird flying high in the sky.
What is it like?
Write about what you can see, feel, smell and hear.

1 The type of place an animal lives in is called its habitat
   or environment.
   Copy the headings below.

2 Write the names of some more animals that live in
   these environments.
   The pictures will help you.

Underground
mole

River/pond
newt

Sky
eagle

ACROSTIC POETRY

Here is a poem about where a bird lives.

Acrostic means
a poem or puzzle
in which the first
(or last) letters
of each line spell
a word.

Blackbird
In the sky
Right up in the clouds
Dancing on the wind

1 Read the first letter of each line going down.
   What do they spell?

Here is a poem about where a fish lives.

Fish below the water
In the gloomy deep.
Swimming, eating, playing,
Hanging still, asleep.

2 Read the first letter of each line going down.
What do they spell?

3 Now you try to write a poem like that for a
CAT or MOLE.

WORKING WITH WORDS

Animal homes have special names.
Copy out the names of the animals and put the right home
next to each.

The first one is done for you:

fox   den

fox   lodge
rabbit   burrow
swallow   hive
badger   den
pig   anthill
beaver   nest
bee   sty
ant   sett

Tigers

Tigers belong to the cat family. They can be found in the cold, snowy environments of Siberia. Here they have long, thick fur to keep them warm. They also live in warm places such as jungles in India.

Tigers do not live in herds or packs like some animals but hunt on their own.

A male tiger is bigger than a female tiger but apart from this they look the same. They have orange fur and black stripes. The stripes help them to hide in the grass and in trees. Some tigers have white fur but there are not many of these in the world.

Tigers rest in the day and hunt at night. They like to catch deer and wild pig but they will eat almost any animal. Tigers are not really fast runners so they have to creep very close to their prey and then pounce.

Glossary

prey means something that is hunted

COMPREHENSION

Read the passage. Copy out the sentences that are true.

1 A female tiger is bigger than a male tiger.

2 Tigers live and hunt alone.

3 Tigers belong to the cat family.

4 Most tigers have orange fur and black stripes.

5 Tigers hunt at night.

6 Tigers will only eat deer and wild pig.

7 Tigers cannot run very fast.

8 Tigers only live in hot environments.

Now look at the sentences you think are not true.
Can you write them and make them true?
The first one is done for you:

1 A female tiger is bigger than a male tiger.
This should say: A male tiger is bigger than a female tiger.

The tiger was hungry. He had not been very good at hunting the last few nights and he really wanted something to eat. He had had a good rest during the hot day and now he was ready to find a meal.

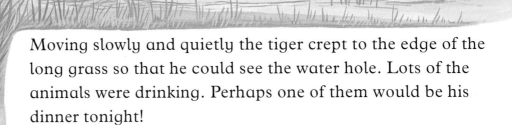

Moving slowly and quietly the tiger crept to the edge of the long grass so that he could see the water hole. Lots of the animals were drinking. Perhaps one of them would be his dinner tonight!

1 Finish the story. These questions will help you.

● What do you think happened next?
● What animal did the tiger hunt?
● Did the tiger get his dinner?
● Did the animals get away?

2 Draw a picture.

Look at the picture carefully.

- Think about what you can see in the picture.
- Think about the colours.
- Think about what the tiger looks like.
- Think about what the tiger is doing.

Write a description of the picture for a friend.

Tropical Storm with a Tiger (Surpris!) by Henri Rousseau Reproduced by courtesy of the Trustees, The National Gallery, London

WORKING WITH WORDS

Look at these animals.

Write a list of the ones that belong to the cat family.

monkey

leopard

jaguar

elephant

giraffe

cheetah

lynx

lion

Down on the farm

Plan of Hill Farm

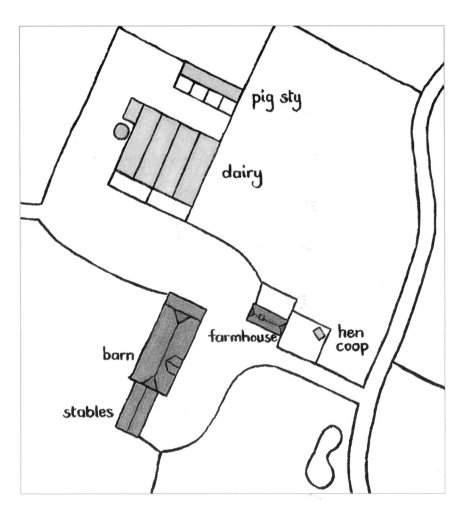

COMPREHENSION

Look at the buildings on the plan.
Answer these questions.

1 Where do the farmer and his family live?

2 Where are the cows milked?

3 Where are the horses kept ?

4 Where do the hens lay their eggs?

5 Where do the pigs live?

6 Where are the crops kept?

USING THE PLAN

Make a list of the buildings you can see on the plan of
the farm.

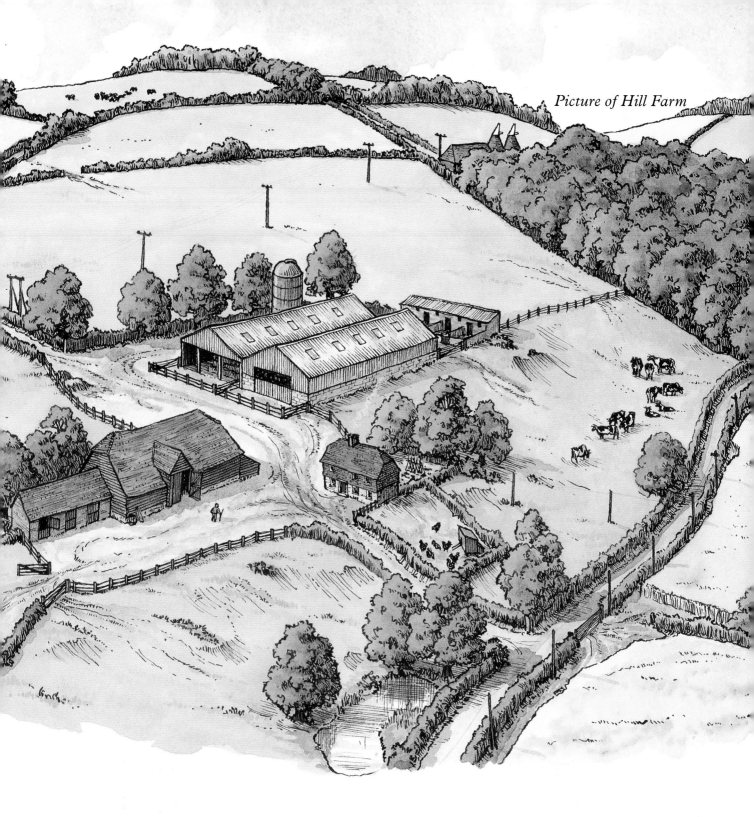

Picture of Hill Farm

COMPREHENSION

1 Make a list of the things you can see in the picture that you cannot see on the plan.

2 Why do you think there are more things in the picture than on the plan?

3 By looking at the stables in the picture, you can see what it is like. Describe the stables.

DESCRIBING A FARMHOUSE

Look at the pictures.
Which farmhouse would you like to live in?

A

B

C

D

E

1 Write about what your farmhouse looks like from the outside.

- What is it made of?
- What colour is it?
- Is it an old building or a new building?

2 Write about the rooms inside your farmhouse.

- How many rooms does it have?
- Which is the biggest room?
- Why would you like to live there?

FARM RULES

Many people like to visit farms.

If you visit a farm there are things you should do and things you should not do.

1 Can you think of a reason for each of these rules?
   The first one is done for you.

2 Now you do the rest. Write a sentence for each rule.

WORKING WITH WORDS

Farmhouse is a compound word. It is made up of two words.

farm + house

Join 'house' to these words and see how many compound words you can make.

top   work   light   boat   bound   hold

Write a sentence for each word.

Weather and seasons

The Months of the Year

January brings the snow;
Makes the toes and fingers glow.

February brings the rain,
Thaws the frozen ponds again.

March brings breezes loud and shrill,
Stirs the dancing daffodil.

April brings the primrose sweet,
Scatters daisies at our feet.

May brings flocks of pretty lambs,
Skipping by their fleecy dams.

June brings tulips, lilies, roses;
Fills the children's hands with posies.

Hot July brings cooling showers,
Strawberries and gilly-flowers.

August brings the sheaves of corn,
Then the Harvest home is borne.

Warm September brings the fruit,
Sportsmen then begin to shoot.

Fresh October brings the pheasant;
Then to gather nuts is pleasant.

Dull November brings the blast
Then the leaves are falling fast.

Chill December brings the sleet,
Blazing fires and Christmas treat.

Glossary
dam is an animal's mother
posies are bunches of flowers
borne means carried
a pheasant is a wild bird with
long tail feathers

Sara Coleridge

COMPREHENSION

Read the poem and answer the questions.

1 In which months do we get sleet or snow?

2 Which are the windy months?

3 Which is the Harvest month?

4 Why do you think October is 'fresh'?

5 Why do you think November is 'dull'?

MAKING LISTS

1 Make a list of all the flowers in the poem.

2 Make a list of all the types of weather in the poem.

DESCRIBING THE SEASONS

You can see some of the things that happen in Spring, Summer, Autumn and Winter in the pictures.

Write about what you can see in each one.

MY FAVOURITE TIME OF YEAR

1 Write about the season you like best. These sentences will help you.

● Think about why you like it.

● Think about what sorts of things you do.

● Think about what sorts of clothes you wear.

2 Write about the season you don't like.

● Why don't you like it?

THE SEASONS

The dotted lines on the chart show you when each season begins and ends.

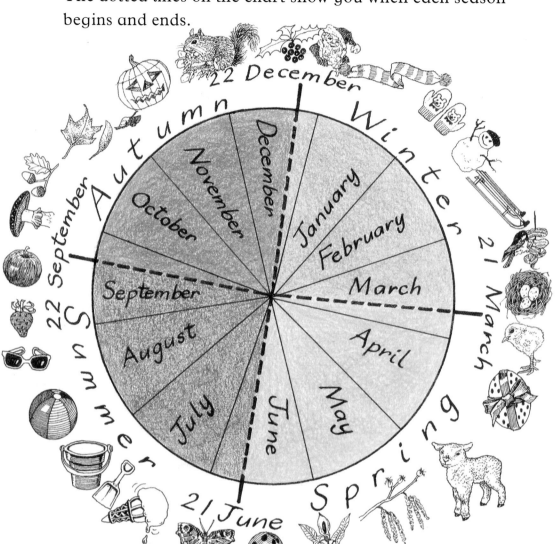

COMPREHENSION

Look carefully at the chart and answer the questions.

1 In which season is April?

2 In which season is July?

3 In which season is February?

4 In which season is your birthday?

5 In which season is Christmas?

6 Which season comes between Autumn and Spring?

7 Do seasons remind you of colours?
Copy these headings into your book.

Spring   Summer   Autumn   Winter

Underneath, write the colours each season reminds **you** of.

18

AN INFORMATION POEM

Thirty days hath September,
April, June and November.
All the rest have thirty-one,
Except for February alone
Which has twenty-eight days clear
And twenty-nine each leap year.

1 The poem tells you how many
days each month has.
Write the names of all the months
down the side of your page.

2 Work out from the poem how many
days are in each month.
The first is done for you:

January has thirty-one days
February
March . . . and so on.

(Remember the capital letters!)

Watch out
for
February!

WORKING WITH WORDS

Homophones are words that have the **same** sound but
different meanings and spelling.

Can you find a homophone for each of these weather words?

weather   blew   rain   sun    mist

19

Looking at pictures

Van Gogh was a famous painter who was born in Holland in 1853.

This is a painting of his bedroom.

'The bedroom at Arles' Vincent Van Gogh Foundation/Van Gogh Museum Amsterdam.

By looking carefully at the painting we can find out some things about him.

COMPREHENSION

Answer these questions in sentences.

1 Did Van Gogh like dark, dull colours or bright colours?

2 Does his room look comfortable or uncomfortable?

3 Did he wear a hat?

4 What do you think he used the blue jug and bowl for?

5 Write a list of things you can see in the room.

6 Write five adjectives to describe the room.

SPOT THE DIFFERENCE

Look at the two pictures.
They look the same in lots of ways but there are some differences.

Picture 2

Picture 1

Talk about the pictures with your friend.
Write a list of the ten things that are different.

COMPREHENSION

Look carefully at the two pictures again.
Answer these questions in sentences.

1 How do you think the man in picture 1 is feeling?

2 How do you think the man in picture 2 is feeling?

3 How do you think the child in picture 1 is feeling?

4 How do you think the child in picture 2 is feeling?

5 What do you think might have happened to the sandcastle in picture 2?

By using words carefully you can help people to see what you are writing about.

These describing words are called **adjectives**. Look:

a dog   a **brown** dog   a **large**, **brown** dog   a **large**, **fierce**, **brown** dog

Now think about a tree.

What **size** is your tree?

● Is it a big tree?

● Is it a small tree?

1 Write a sentence about the **size** of your tree.

What **shape** is your tree?

● Is it a thin tree?

● Is it a bushy tree?

● Is it a straight tree?

● Is it a bent tree?

2 Write a sentence about the **shape** of your tree.

What **colour** is your tree?

● Are the leaves green?

● Are the leaves brown?

● Is it a tree with blossom?

● Is it a tree with fruit?

● Is it a tree with berries?

3 Write a sentence about the **colour** of your tree.

What are the **leaves** like on your tree?

- Are the leaves long and thin?
- Are the leaves short?
- Are there lots of leaves?
- Has your tree lost its leaves?

4 Write a sentence about the **leaves** on your tree.

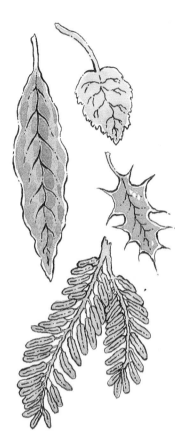

Now you have used words to paint a picture of your tree.
Draw and colour your tree.
Think about where your tree is.

- Is it in a garden?
- Is it in a wood?
- Is it by itself?
- Is it with other trees?

5 Write about **where** your tree is.

WORKING WITH WORDS

Colours come in different shades.
Two people might have brown hair:

  one has copper-coloured hair
  one has mousey-brown hair.

They are both shades of brown.

These are shades of red, green or yellow:

lemon   emerald   scarlet   lime

maroon   pink   mustard   crimson   gold

Put these words under the correct heading below.
Use a dictionary for the words you have not seen before.

red   green   yellow

Sounds around us

Wind Song

When the wind blows
The quiet things speak.
Some whisper, some clang,
some creak.

Grasses swish.
Treetops sigh.
Flags slap
and snap at the sky.
Wires on poles
whistle and hum.
Ashcans roll.
Windows drum.

When the wind goes –
suddenly
then,
the quiet things
are quiet again.

Lilian Moore

Glossary *ashcan* means dustbin

COMPREHENSION   Read the poem and answer the questions.

1 What is making a swishing noise?

2 What whistle and hum?

3 Find two words in the poem that describe a loud noise.

4 Can you think of any more loud words?

5 Find two words in the poem that describe a quiet noise.

6 Can you think of any more quiet words?

WEATHER SOUNDS

Sometimes we make words from the sound they describe, like the grass 'swishing'.

These 'sound' words are called onomatopoeic words.

The poem has lots of sound words in it.

You can hear the sounds when the wind blows.

What sounds can you hear when it is raining?

The picture will help you to write some of the 'sound' words.

Can you find any more?

trickling

pounding

dripping

splashing

There are lots of words for all sorts of sounds.

An old door **creaks**.
A telephone **rings**.
People can **shout**, **mumble**, **sing**, **moan** (and lots of others).

Look at the pictures.
- Which words describe the sounds the people are making?
- Which words describe the sounds in the other pictures?

1 Write a sentence for each picture describing the sound.
   The first is done for you.

The woman is whispering.

An Evening at Alfie's

Alfie's Mum and Dad have gone to a party. Maureen is babysitting and she reads Alfie a bedtime story.

Tonight Alfie wanted the story about Noah and his Ark full of animals. Alfie liked to hear how the rain came drip, drip, drip, and then splash! splash! splash! and then rushing everywhere, until the whole world was covered with water.

When Maureen had finished the story it was time for Alfie to go to bed . . . Alfie didn't feel sleepy. He lay in bed looking at the patch of light on the ceiling. For a long time all was quiet. Then he heard a funny noise outside on the landing.

Alfie sat up. The noise was just outside his door. Drip, drip, drip! Soon it got quicker. It changed to drip-drip, drip-drip, drip-drip! It was getting louder too.

Alfie got out of bed and peeped round the door. There was a puddle on the floor. He looked up. Water was splashing into the puddle from the ceiling, drip-drip, drip-drip, drip-drip! It was raining inside the house!

Shirley Hughes

NIGHT SOUNDS

Alfie could not sleep because of the dripping sound he could hear.

1 Think about when you are in bed at night.

- What sounds can you hear inside the house?
- Is someone moving around?
- Can you hear the television or radio?
- Is someone getting washed?
- What sounds can you hear outside?
- Can you hear traffic?
- Can you hear the wind or rain?
- Have you ever heard any unusual noises like Alfie did?

2 Write about the sounds you hear and the things and people that make those sounds.

WORKING WITH WORDS

KERPOW!

There are twenty-six letters in the alphabet.
Five of the letters are vowels a e i o u.
Twenty-one are consonants. Write down the twenty-one consonants and find a sound word which starts with each letter. Use your dictionary to help you.
Make up a word if you really get stuck!

Chinese dragons

There are two very important Chinese festivals and both are to do with dragons.

Chinese dragons bring good luck. Long ago people believed that the dragons lived in the clouds and brought the rain.

The Spring festival marks the Chinese New Year. People dress up in dragon costumes and dance through the streets. Children throw buckets of water at the dancers shouting, 'Here comes the rain!'. Families always try to be together at New Year and fireworks are let off to scare away evil spirits.

In the Dragon Boat festival, boats decorated with dragon heads race each other and rice is thrown on the water.

Read the passage and answer the questions.

1 What are the names of two important Chinese festivals?

2 Why were dragons thought to be lucky?

3 What happens at New Year in China?

4 What happens at the Dragon Boat festival?

MY DRAGON COSTUME

Imagine you are going to be part of the Spring festival.
Write about your dragon costume.
The pictures here will help you.

- What will it be made of?
- Remember that you have to wear it so it can't be too heavy.
- What colours will it be?
- Will the face show a friendly dragon or an angry dragon?
- The dragon head is very big.
  How will you see where you are going?

There's no such thing as a dragon by *Jack Kent*

Billy Bixbee was rather surprised when he woke up one morning and found a dragon in his room. It was a small dragon, about the size of a kitten. . . . Billy went downstairs to tell his mother.

'There's no such thing as a dragon,' said Billy's mother.

Billy went back to his room and began to dress. . . . He washed his face and hands and went down to breakfast. The dragon went, too. It was bigger now, almost the size of a dog. . . . Mother made some pancakes for Billy, but the dragon ate them all. Mother made some more. But the dragon ate those, too. . . .

Billy went upstairs to brush his teeth. Mother started clearing the table. The dragon, who was quite as big as Mother by this time, made himself comfortable on the hall rug and went to sleep.

By the time Billy came back downstairs the dragon had grown so much he filled the hall. Billy had to go around by way of the living room to get to where his mother was. 'I didn't know dragons grew so fast!' said Billy.

'There's no such thing as a dragon!' said Mother firmly. . . .

By mid-day the dragon filled the house. Its head hung out of the front door, its tail hung out of the back door, and there wasn't a room in the house that didn't have some part of the dragon in it.

COMPREHENSION   Read the passage and answer the questions.

1 Why do you think the dragon kept growing?

2 Do you agree with Billy's mother that there is no such thing as a dragon?

3 If you found a dragon in your bedroom would the other people in your house believe you?

4 There are lots of stories and poems about dragons. Make a list of as many as you can find.

FINISH THE STORY
- Do you think the dragon kept on growing?
- What happened?
- Did Billy manage to get the dragon back to its normal size?
- How did he do this?
- Did Mother believe in the dragon in the end?

China has many languages but the one that most people speak is called Standard Chinese. Chinese writing is made up of pictures. Look:

English	Standard Chinese	How we would write it	How we would say it
one	壹	yi	yee
two	貳	er	ur
three	叁	san	sahn
four	肆	si	see
five	伍	wu	woo
six	陸	liu	leo
seven	柒	qi	chee
eight	捌	ba	bah
nine	玖	jiu	jeo
ten	拾	shi	she

1 How many things can you see in each picture?

2 Write the number as the Chinese would.

3 Write the number as we would.

Houses and homes

The Mice who Lived in a Shoe

This is a story about a shoe . . . and the family of mice who lived in it.
When it rained they got wet. When it snowed they got cold. When the
sun shone, they got hot. When the wind blew, they flew all over the place.
But the worst thing of all was when the cat put his paw into the shoe
and stretched out his claws. The family huddled together at the toe end
for safety. They all squeaked until the cat went away.

When they were sure the cat had gone,
they gathered round Ma in the dark.

'The only way to be safe from the cat and to
shelter from the weather,' said Pa, 'is to build a house.'

'Where, where?' the family cried.

'Right here, in this shoe,' replied Pa.

'What a good idea,' said Ma, 'I'll
make the curtains.'

'There'll be other things to
do before that,' observed Grandpa.

Pa asked everyone to draw their
dream house. There was a big house,
a small house, a short house, a tall
house, a fat house, a thin house,
a long house, a red house, a blue
house and a green house.

Pa looked at them carefully
to see who had the best ideas.
Then he drew their
dream house.

Rodney Peppé

COMPREHENSION   Read the passage and answer the questions.

1 What were the two things that the shoe did not keep out?

2 What did the mice decide to do about it?

3 What do you think Pa meant when he asked them to draw their 'dream house'?

4 Grandpa said they had 'other things' to do before they could put up the curtains. Make a list of the things you think the mice had to do to build their dream house.

5 What makes a house a home?

DESCRIBING HOMES   Look at these homes.

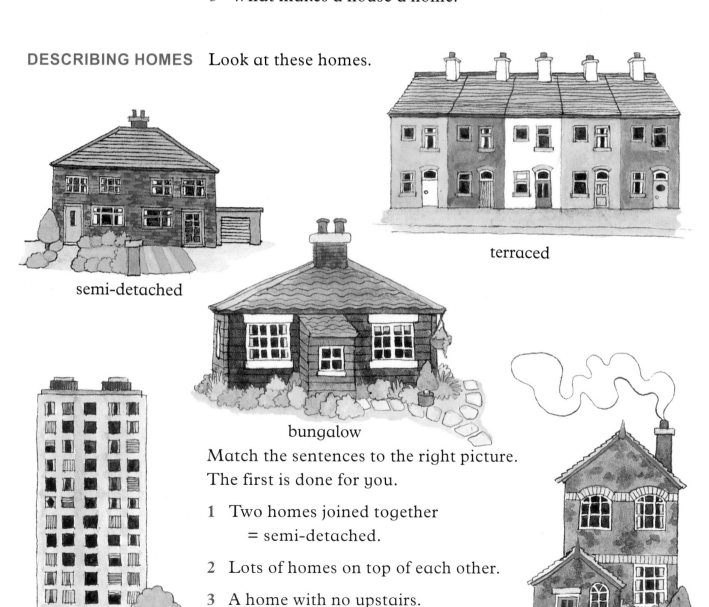

semi-detached

terraced

bungalow

Match the sentences to the right picture.
The first is done for you.

1 Two homes joined together
   = semi-detached.

2 Lots of homes on top of each other.

3 A home with no upstairs.

4 A home on its own.

5 Lots of homes joined together.

block of flats

detached

These pictures show you different sorts of homes.
Choose the right ending for each sentence.

1 Some people in Bangkok have houses on stilts because

   a they like living high up.
   b they build their houses over water.
   c there is a lot of snow.

2 Some people in Africa make their houses out of mud
   because

   a they don't like bricks.
   b mud bakes hard in the hot sun.
   c it keeps the cold out.

3 Bedouin people in the desert live in tents because

   a it rains a lot.

   b they don't like walls.

   c they move from place to place.

4 Some people in Hong Kong live in junks because

   a there is not much land in Hong Kong to build on.

   b they are all sailors.

   c they like swimming.

Imagine you are living in one of these homes.

Make a list of the things you would like about living there.

Make a list of the things you would miss.

WORKING WITH WORDS

Lots of people help to build our homes.

architect   bricklayer   plumber   carpenter   plasterer   electrician

Write a sentence about each one saying what they do.

Use a dictionary to help you.

People in our community

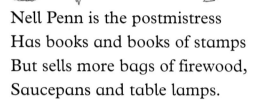

Business

Dick Hambone is a grocer,
Who sells tinned fruit and rice,
He weighs the cheese by ounces,
Puts pennies on the price.

Ann Packet has a sweet shop
And lives on chocolate drops,
She'll eat up all the profits
If nibbling never stops.

And Peter Blood the butcher,
He calls my mother, 'Ma'am',
And gives her best New Zealand
When she wants English lamb.

Nell Penn is the postmistress
Has books and books of stamps
But sells more bags of firewood,
Saucepans and table lamps.

Tom Salmon, our fishmonger
Washes his marble slabs
And chops the heads off herrings
And fillets plaice and dabs.

Leonard Clark

Glossary
dabs are flat fish

COMPREHENSION   Read the poem and answer the questions.

1 What could you buy from Dick Hambone?

2 What could you buy from Ann Packet?

3 What could you buy from Peter Blood?

4 What could you buy from Nell Penn?

5 What could you buy from Tom Salmon?

6 Look at the names of the shopkeepers.
   Do you notice anything about them?

DESCRIBING SHOPS   Look at the pictures.

1   What kind of shop is the first one?

2   Do you have this kind of shop near you?

3   What sorts of things can you buy there?

4   What kind of shop is the second one?

5   Do you have this kind of shop near you?

6   What sorts of things can you buy there?

WRITING ABOUT JOBS   These people also do jobs in your community.
All these jobs are important.

1   Write a sentence for each picture saying what these people do.

2   Write about the kind of job you would like to do or a job you would
not like to do. Remember to say why!

There are lots of places in the community where people go to enjoy themselves. Look at the pictures.

Match the words below with the right pictures.
The first is done for you.

A is a swimming pool

library   bowling alley   cinema

park   swimming pool   restaurant

Answer these questions in sentences.

1 What would you wear in the swimming pool?

2 What would you see at the cinema?

3 What would you do in the park?

4 Why would you go to a library?

5 What would you do in a bowling alley?

6 What would you get in a restaurant?

Have you ever been to any of these places?
Choose one of the places and write about it.
These questions will help you.

● Why did you go there?
● Was it a special treat?
● What did you do there?
● Did you like it?
● Did you go with your family?
● Did you go with a friend?

WORKING WITH WORDS

People live in different sorts of communities.

1 What do you think is the difference between:
a village
a town
a city?

Use your dictionary to help you.

2 Do you live in a village, a town or a city?
Write the name of the place where you live.
How long has your family lived there?

Romans in Britain

The Romans were the first people to build roads in Britain. They needed strong, straight roads to move goods from one place to another, and for the Roman army to march quickly to places where there was trouble.

The Romans built their roads by first digging a ditch. They put large stones in the bottom of the ditch. They then put smaller stones in, and on top of the smaller stones they put gravel. At the very top they put paving stones.

COMPREHENSION   Read the passage, look at the map, and answer the questions.

1 Why did the Romans need strong, straight roads?
2 Which road went from Dover to Chester?
3 Which road went from Exeter to Lincoln?
4 Which road went from London to York?

INSTRUCTIONS FOR BUILDING A ROMAN ROAD

Read the passage about Roman roads again.
In your book, draw a ditch like this.

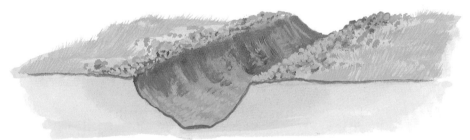

Now draw the things in the ditch that the Romans used to
build their roads.
You have to put them in the ditch in the right order!
There are four things to draw in your ditch.
Begin with the large stones.

When you have finished the drawing, write about how you
would make the road. Begin like this:

1 Dig a ditch.

41

HADRIAN'S WALL

The Romans settled in many parts of Britain but they did not settle in Scotland. A tribe of people called the Picts lived there and they were good fighters. The Romans could not beat them.

One of the Roman leaders in Britain called Hadrian decided to build a wall to stop the Picts attacking them. It took 10,000 soldiers to guard the wall. Hadrian's Wall was 73 miles long. Every 5 miles there was a fort that could house hundreds of soldiers.

COMPREHENSION

Read the passage and answer the questions.

1 Who lived in Scotland in Roman times?

2 Whose idea was it to build the wall?

3 Why did he want to build the wall?

4 How many soldiers were needed to guard the wall?

5 How long was the wall?

6 Where did the soldiers who guarded the wall live?

This is a photograph of Hadrian's Wall as it is today.

MY LIFE AS A SOLDIER

Imagine you are a Roman soldier who is guarding the wall in winter.

Write a letter home to tell your family what it is like.

These ideas will help you

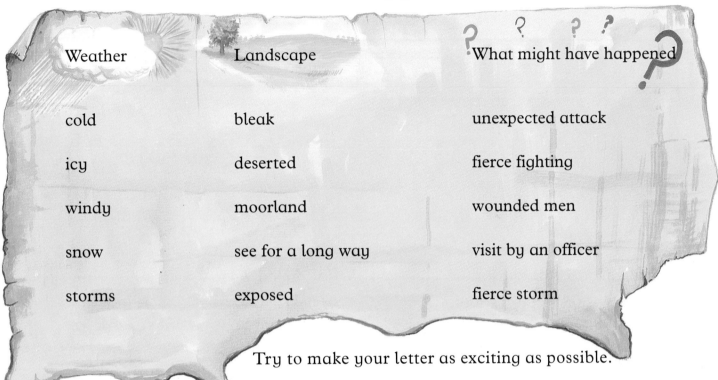

Weather	Landscape	What might have happened
cold	bleak	unexpected attack
icy	deserted	fierce fighting
windy	moorland	wounded men
snow	see for a long way	visit by an officer
storms	exposed	fierce storm

Try to make your letter as exciting as possible.

WORKING WITH WORDS

The Romans had their own way of writing numbers.

1 = I		6 = VI
2 = II		7 = VII
3 = III		8 = VIII
4 = IV		9 = IX
5 = V		10 = X

How would the Romans have written the answers to these sums?

4 + 3 =
5 + 4 =
6 + 2 =
1 + 3 =
9 + 1 =
2 + 3 =

Can you find out the Roman way of writing 50 and 100?

The legend of King Arthur

Long ago lived a wise old wizard called Merlin. He could see what was going to happen in the future. He could work magic spells.

Merlin's friend, King Uther, had a baby son called Arthur. Merlin knew that some knights wanted to be king after Uther died. They would try to kill Arthur. Merlin took the baby away. He asked a trusted knight, Sir Ector, to look after him. He did not tell Sir Ector that Arthur was the king's son.

When Uther died, the knights fought each other to see who would be king. No one but Merlin knew Uther had a son.

Merlin thought it was time that Arthur should be king. All the knights were invited to London to see who could pull the sword out of a big stone. The one who could do it would be king.

Sir Ector, his real son Sir Kay, and Arthur went to London. None of the knights could pull the sword out of the stone.

Arthur stepped forward and, to everyone's surprise, pulled the sword from the stone and was crowned king.

Glossary

knights were men who dressed in armour and fought on horseback

COMPREHENSION   Answer these questions in sentences.

1 Who was Arthur's real father?

2 Who took Arthur away?

3 Who looked after Arthur as a boy?

4 How do you think Sir Ector felt when he saw Arthur with the sword?

5 How do you think the other knights felt when they saw Arthur with the sword?

DESCRIBING MERLIN

Merlin was the magician who helped Arthur.
Imagine you were describing Merlin to a friend
who had not seen the picture.
Write a description of Merlin by looking carefully
at the picture.

- What is he wearing?

- What pictures are on his clothes?

- What does his hat look like?

- What is he carrying?

- What sort of person do you think Merlin is?

MY DAY AS KING OR QUEEN

Imagine you could be king or queen for one day.

- You could change rules and make up new ones.

- You could go anywhere you wanted to.

- What rules would you change?

- Where would you go?

Write about the things you would do
if you were king or queen for a day.

To advertise something is to tell people all about it.
Here is a poster advertising the sword in the stone.

The words on the poster tell us something about:

What has to be done.

Who is invited to try.

What will happen to the person who can pull the sword out of the stone.

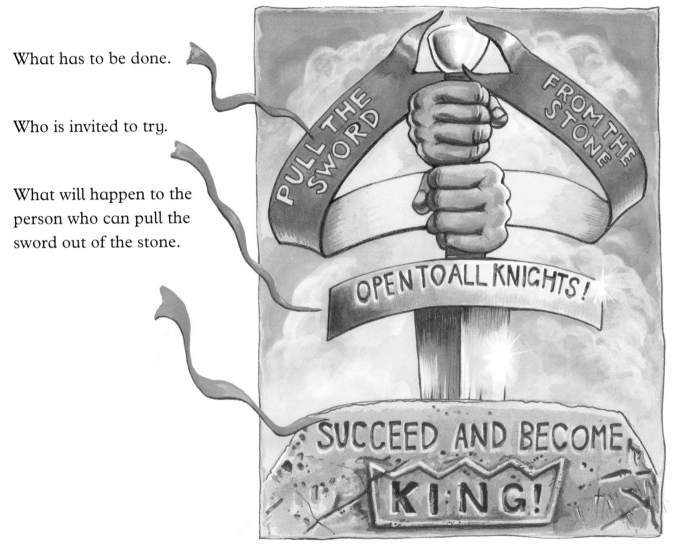

1 Think about another competition for the knights to try.
Draw a poster to show:
What has to be done.
Who can try and
what the winner will get.

Remember you want people to stop and read your poster.
Make it bright and colourful.
Make the words on your poster easy to read.

Many of our words have come from Anglo-Saxon times.
Here are some that are very like the ones we use today.

Copy the pictures and write the names the way we write them today.
Do you know these words in any other language?